How I Settled the

WEST

by Sharon Fear
illustrated by Doron Putka

MODERN CURRICULUM PRESS
Pearson Learning Group

Early one morning, right about dawn, I decided to go out and settle the West.

I had been hearing for quite some time about how folks were trying to settle it. Why hadn't they gotten the job done yet? I couldn't for the life of me figure it out. I made up my mind to leave that very day and go get it settled, once and for all.

My darling husband, a sailor, was out to sea at the time. So I left him a letter telling him to come and find us—me and the children—when he finally docked. I told him we'd gone on out west to get some land. I figured we would clear it, build a cabin, and get a crop in. We'd have things shipshape when he arrived.

I loaded all of our worldly belongings into the wagon, hitched up the oxen, and tied the saddle horse behind. I rounded up the children, of which I had only six at the time. Away we went, rumbling and rocking down the trail.

Somewhere along the way we acquired a young coyote that followed along as loyally as a dog.

When sunset came, we'd make our camp by a riverbank and go catch supper. I'd slip off my shoes and stockings and run down a rabbit. My oldest daughter, who was almost as quick as I am, would catch us a fish or two with her bare hands.

The children taught the coyote a little tune— I forget which one—and it sang along with us every night in a fine voice.

So we found ourselves with good company, plenty to eat, and lots of singing around the campfire. The singing made me a little sorrowful sometimes, but I just ignored that. All in all, we were having a splendid journey.

But one day a stranger stepped out of the woods. I knew right off he was up to no good.

"Hold up there!" he shouted out. "Well, now, little lady, is it just you and the children?

"Yes, sir," I replied. I tried to be civil to everyone—even to a fellow who looked as if he'd been chewing hickory nuts and spitting into the wind.

"I'll just have that pouch that's hanging at your waist there, and the coins in it," he growled. "And don't give me any trouble. I'm a dangerous man!"

So I untied the purse from my belt and held it out. But, mercy me, I dropped it! Just then the wagon bumped forward a bit and a wheel came to rest on the purse.

"I'll get it," I said. I jumped down and lifted the wagon up with one hand while I got the purse with the other.

"By thunder!" I heard the robber say.

"It feels as if that big old wagon wheel bent these little coins," I said. And I took out one and bent it back into shape with my thumb. "There, now, I've straightened that one out for you."

But when I looked up and held out the coins, the fellow was gone!

That was the only annoying thing that happened the whole time—if you don't count the forest fire and the buffalo stampede— before we finally arrived in Paradise.

Paradise, Texas, to be precise. There were long, grassy meadows and sparkling waters and some fine big trees. The whole family joined hands and reached around the trunk of one, and we couldn't close the circle.

"I'll have to have some more children," I said, and we all laughed.

Then I took off my shoes and stockings and climbed that tree to find out if it had a top. All those trees were so tall that the tops just disappeared into the clouds.

After some climbing I did finally reach the top. I sat there for a while admiring the view. But then I saw a few snowflakes in the air, and I knew we'd better start building.

That afternoon we cut down a tree. Just one of the bigger saplings was enough. Then we got busy building. We threw up a barn and corral for the animals, and a pleasant cabin for ourselves. By that evening the children, the coyote, and I were singing songs in our own little parlor in front of our own blazing fireplace.

And just in time too!

The snow fell and the river froze. We moved the oxen and the horse into the parlor. It was mighty crowded, but also warmer. And we now had a couple of bass voices to improve our nightly entertainment. I still felt sad, like something was missing. But I sang along, just as loud as a bell.

When the fire went out, it got very cold. It wasn't until we couldn't sing another note that I got worried. When we tried to speak, our words froze solid in the air. Then they fell to the ground and shattered.

I knew I had to do something. So I went out and found a bear asleep in her den. Then I woke her up.

While she was still groggy and not thinking straight, I spoke up. "Poor thing," I said. "You're sure not ready for winter, are you?" She just blinked at me. "That coat of yours is mighty thin," I said. "I can see your bare hide peeking through the fur there."

The bear looked down at itself.

"Why, the elbows are out, and it looks as if you've got a seam parting. Right here," I said. "And something has splattered on the back and left a nasty big stain."

The bear's brow wrinkled up. She turned her head and tried to look at her back.

"Tell you what I'll do," I said. And I talked her out of her fur coat. I didn't leave her naked to the elements, naturally. In exchange for her coat, I gave her a good thick blanket and a pair of good, thick wool stockings.

When I had done this to four or five more
bears, I had enough fur coats to keep the
whole family warm through the winter.

Then one day the snow was gone. The river
flowed free again, and the sun felt warm on
our faces. Buds were swelling on the trees, and
little green things pushed up out of the ground.

"Children and coyote," I said, "spring is
here. It's time to plant."

But when I looked out at that land, there
must have been about a thousand acres. I
wondered how I was going to get it all plowed
with just four oxen.

As I gave it some thought, I began to recall something that had happened on the journey.

I called my oldest son and told him what to do. He saddled the horse and rode off, taking the coyote with him.

Meanwhile, the rest of the children and I cut down another sapling. Out of this we made rails. We fenced in the cabin, the barn, the garden, and anything else that we didn't want destroyed.

Just as we finished, we heard the mighty thundering.

My boy and the coyote stampeded a herd of buffalo clear across the homestead. In about ten minutes, their hooves had churned up that whole thousand acres just right.

As soon as the herd was off in the distance, I sent the children out to plant. I could tell the soil was rich. Plants were sprouting up almost as soon as the seed hit the ground.

While the children worked, I looked out over the field already turning to wheat, the new fences, the barn and corral, and our snug little cabin.

"There," I said to myself. "That's all settled."

I felt right proud of it all.

But something was nagging at me too. For I was getting that sorrowful feeling again. Something was still missing.

Right then, I heard the shout.

"Ahoy, sweetheart!"

"Darling!" I cried. And I ran to embrace my husband.

"What a trim little place!" he said, looking in the parlor window. "Did you and the children have any trouble?"

Well, I had to laugh. "You know better than that!" I said. "Settling the West was no bother at all."

That night, as the family was singing, I felt downright happy. My husband's deep voice filled our little parlor. Only then did I know what I had missed so much. I think next time I tame a new land, I'll just let him tag along.